A LIFEGUIDE BIBLE STUDY

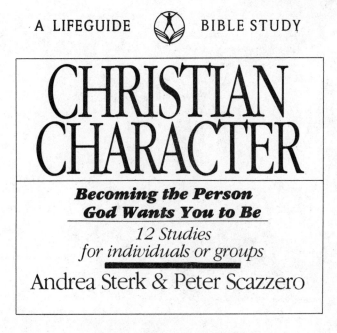

CHRISTIAN CHARACTER

**Becoming the Person
God Wants You to Be**

*12 Studies
for individuals or groups*

Andrea Sterk & Peter Scazzero

With Notes for Leaders

INTERVARSITY PRESS
DOWNERS GROVE, ILLINOIS 60515

InterVarsity Press is the book-publishing division of Inter-Varsity Christian Fellowship, a student movement active on campus at hundreds of universities, colleges and schools of nursing. For information about local and regional activities, write IVCF, 233 Langdon St., Madison, WI 53703.

Distributed in Canada through InterVarsity Press, 860 Denison St., Unit 3, Markham, Ontario L3R 4H1, Canada.

All Scripture quotations, unless otherwise indicated, are taken from the Holy Bible, New International Version. Copyright © 1973, 1978 International Bible Society. Used by permission of Zondervan Bible Publishers.

Cover photograph: Robert McKendrick

ISBN 0-8308-1054-4

Printed in the United States of America

20	19	18	17	16	15	14	13	12	11	10	9
99	98	97	96	95	94	93	92	91	90	89	

Contents

Getting the Most
from LifeGuide Bible Studies

Many of us long to fill our minds and our lives with Scripture. We desire to be transformed by its message. LifeGuide Bible Studies are designed to be an exciting and challenging way to do just that. They help us to be guided by God's Word in every area of life.

How They Work

LifeGuides have a number of distinctive features. Perhaps the most important is that they are *inductive* rather than *deductive*. In other words, they lead us to *discover* what the Bible says rather than simply *telling* us what it says.

They are also thought provoking. They help us to think about the meaning of the passage so that we can truly understand what the author is saying. The questions require more than one-word answers.

The studies are personal. Questions expose us to the promises, assurances, exhortations and challenges of God's Word. They are designed to allow the Scriptures to renew our minds so that we can be transformed by the Spirit of God. This is the ultimate goal of all Bible study.

The studies are versatile. They are designed for student, neighborhood and church groups. They are also effective for individual study.

How They're Put Together

LifeGuides also have a distinctive format. Each study need take no more than forty-five minutes in a group setting or thirty minutes in personal study—unless you choose to take more time.

The studies can be used within a quarter system in a church and fit well in a semester or trimester system on a college campus. If a guide has more than thirteen studies, it is divided into two or occasionally three parts of approximately twelve studies each.

LifeGuides use a workbook format. Space is provided for writing answers to each question. This is ideal for personal study and allows group members to prepare in advance for the discussion.

The studies also contain leader's notes. They show how to lead a group discussion, provide additional background information on certain questions, give helpful tips on group dynamics and suggest ways to deal with problems which may arise during the discussion. With such helps, someone with little or no experience can lead an effective study.

Suggestions for Individual Study

1. As you begin each study, pray that God will help you to understand and apply the passage to your life.

2. Read and reread the assigned Bible passage to familiarize yourself with what the author is saying. In the case of book studies, you may want to read through the entire book prior to the first study. This will give you a helpful overview of its contents.

3. A good modern translation of the Bible, rather than the King James Version or a paraphrase, will give you the most help. The New International Version, the New American Standard Bible and the Revised Standard Version are all recommended. However, the questions in this guide are based on the New International Version.

4. Write your answers in the space provided in the study guide. This will help you to express your understanding of the passage clearly.

5. It might be good to have a Bible dictionary handy. Use it to look up any unfamiliar words, names or places.

Suggestions for Group Study

1. Come to the study prepared. Follow the suggestions for individual study mentioned above. You will find that careful preparation will greatly enrich your time spent in group discussion.

2. Be willing to participate in the discussion. The leader of your group will not be lecturing. Instead, he or she will be encouraging the members of the group to discuss what they have learned from the passage. The leader will be asking the questions that are found in this guide. Plan to share what God has taught you in your individual study.

3. Stick to the passage being studied. Your answers should be based on the verses which are the focus of the discussion and not on outside authorities such as commentaries or speakers. This guide deliberately avoids jumping from book to book or passage to passage. Each study focuses on only one passage. Book studies are generally designed to lead you through the book in the order in which it was written. This will help you follow the author's argument.

4. Be sensitive to the other members of the group. Listen attentively when they share what they have learned. You may be surprised by their insights! Link what you say to the comments of others so the group stays on the topic. Also, be affirming whenever you can. This will encourage some of the more hesitant members of the group to participate.

5. Be careful not to dominate the discussion. We are sometimes so eager to share what we have learned that we leave too little opportunity for others to respond. By all means participate! But allow others to also.

6. Expect God to teach you through the passage being discussed and through the other members of the group. Pray that you will have an enjoyable and profitable time together.

7. If you are the discussion leader, you will find additional suggestions and helpful ideas for each study in the leader's notes. These are found at the back of the guide.

Introducing Christian Character

Justin Martyr, Augustine of Hippo, John Wycliffe, Martin Luther, John Calvin, Jonathan Edwards, John Wesley, George Whitefield, Dwight L. Moody, Martin Luther King, Billy Graham. All of these people were anointed by God in an extraordinary way and endowed with "spectacular" gifts which caused them to stand out from rank-and-file Christians. They were, and continue to be, greatly used to advance the kingdom of God.

At the same time there have been millions throughout the world who have lived godly lives and yet have died in virtual obscurity. The Moravian Christians are a striking example. By their deep piety and good works, they profoundly influenced John Wesley prior to his conversion. Traveling from England to the United States in 1736, Wesley recorded his impressions of these Moravians in his journal:

> At seven I went to the Germans [Moravians]. I had long before observed the great seriousness of their behaviour. Of their humility they had given a continual proof, by performing those servile offices for the other passengers which none of the English would undertake; . . . If they were pushed, struck, or thrown down, they rose again and went away; but no complaint was found in their mouth. [Wesley's Journal, 1: 142, quoted in Howard Snyder, *The Radical Wesley* (Downers Grove, Ill.: InterVarsity Press, 1980), p. 26.]

But now, 250 years later, who has ever heard of these faithful men and women?

From Timothy's mother and grandmother in the first century (2 Tim 1:3; 3:14-15) to Eric Liddell in the twentieth century, history abounds with such little-known men and women of faith who by their exemplary, Christlike character shaped the history of the church while remaining behind the scenes.

This study guide, entitled *Christian Character,* has been written to awaken us to the character of a true disciple and move us to hunger and thirst after righteousness. The effectiveness of our deeds in the world is determined by the holiness of our lives. But today our standard is often far too mediocre, a standard which has been lowered to enable us to live comfortably. Jesus, however, calls us to live in a counterculture which speaks a prophetic message to the world by its very existence. He demands nothing less of us than perfection (Mt 5:48).

The purpose of this guide is to help us grow in godly character. Toward this end we have prepared twelve inductive Bible studies. Several studies deal with basic yet profound truths undergirding the Christian life (such as justification and lordship). Others focus on those qualities which characterize the life of a disciple (holiness, faith, servanthood). Still others explore specific and often-neglected topics related to Christian character (such as temptation, self-image and spiritual gifts). While the study of Christian character tends to be elusive and ethereal, we have sought to cover each topic in a practical and relevant manner. Although the studies are arranged in a reasonable sequence, please feel free to change the order of the studies to meet your own particular needs.

Through contact with the living Christ, the character of men and women throughout history has been transformed. John, a son of thunder, became the apostle of love. Paul, a hardened persecutor of God's people, gradually took on the gentleness of "a mother caring for her little children" (1 Thess 2:7). May these studies bring you into vital contact with our heavenly Father who promises to conform us to the image of his Son.

1
Justification: The Meaning of the Cross
Romans 3:9-26

We all have a need for acceptance. In fact our self-concept is often determined by the approval or rejection of those around us, whether family, peers, business associates, fellow students or even Christian friends. We tend to do and say what we hope will win people's favor.

This tendency often carries over into our relationship with God. We feel we must somehow earn God's acceptance of us, so we end up acting out of a sense of guilt. In the book of Romans, Paul expounds the doctrine of justification, the biblical foundation upon which a right relationship is built—with ourselves, with others and with God. It frees us to be all that God intends for us.

1. What are some ways we try to earn God's approval?

2. Read Romans 3:9-26. In verses 10-18 Paul cites several Old Testament passages to illustrate the fact that everyone is "under sin" (v. 9). What portrait of humanity emerges from these verses?

3. How does Paul use the various parts of the body to graphically illustrate the extent and effects of sin (vv. 13-18)?

4. Romans 2:5 says there will be a day when God's "righteous judgment will be revealed." What does 3:19-20 indicate about the nature and outcome of that trial?

5. Why must Paul expose our true moral and spiritual condition before he discusses the good news of Jesus Christ?

6. Verses 21-26 introduce several key words which help us to understand the nature of salvation. These include *faith, justified, redemption* and *sacrifice of atonement.* Explain what it means to have faith in Christ (v. 22).

7. The word *justified* (v. 24) is borrowed from the law court. A justified person has no legal charges against him. He is righteous in the eyes of the law. Why is our justification remarkable given our spiritual and moral condition?

---

8. How should a proper understanding of justification affect our self-image?

---

9. The word *redemption* (v. 24) is borrowed from the slave market. It means to buy someone out of slavery. What are some of the ways we were enslaved as non-Christians?

How should the price Jesus paid for our redemption affect our desire to obey him?

---

10. The expression *sacrifice of atonement* (v. 25) is taken from the Old Testament sacrificial system. The death of a sacrificial animal turned away God's wrath from the sinner. How does this imagery help us to understand and appreciate what Jesus did for us on the cross?

11. How should the fact that God has accepted and forgiven us through Christ affect our relationships with one another and with God?

---

12. Take time now to praise God for his loving and costly acceptance of us through Christ.

2
The Lordship of Jesus Christ (Part 1)

Colossians 1:15-23

To some, Jesus of Nazareth is a revolutionary, leading the masses in their struggle for freedom from oppression. Others see him as a staunch conservative, fully supporting and representing the status quo. Still others view Jesus as a pious, meek and mild do-gooder who loves everyone and avoids confrontation at all costs.

What is Jesus really like? Confusion about the identity and character of Jesus was also a problem in the first century. From both inside and outside the church, distortions of the truth about Jesus and the Christian life had arisen. Against this background, Paul writes to the Christians at Colossae, reminding them of who it is they follow as Lord.

1. How did you view Jesus before you became a Christian?

2. Read Colossians 1:15-23. According to verse 15, "Christ is the visible expression of the invisible God" (Phillips). What are some of the difficulties we have in trying to know and relate to an invisible God?

How has Christ's incarnation overcome these difficulties?

3. Christ is also "the firstborn," which means the one who is first (or Lord) over all creation (v. 15). In what ways are his lordship and supremacy indicated in verses 16-20?

4. How does this portrait of Christ enlarge your view of him?

5. According to verse 16, what is the purpose of all created things: nature, people, "rulers" and "authorities"?

How should this affect our attitude toward life—including our possessions, relationships and goals?

6. Christ is also "the head of the body, the church" (v. 18). How should Christ's authority make a visible difference in your church or fellowship group?

7. How does verse 20 help us to understand God's overall plan and goal for the universe?

8. According to verses 21-22, what has God done to enable us to participate in his plan?

What kind of response does he expect from us (v. 23)?

9. Verse 18 summarizes the overall thrust of this passage: "So that in everything he might have the supremacy." In what areas does Jesus not yet have first place in your life?

What steps can you take to submit these areas to his lordship?

10. How can this passage encourage you to "continue in your faith, established and firm, not moved from the hope held out in the gospel" (v. 23)?

3
The Lordship of Jesus Christ (Part 2)

Luke 14:25-35

O ver one billion people today—almost one-fourth of the world's population—call themselves Christians. In the first century, too, multitudes flocked to Jesus. They came for various reasons and with various expectations: to satisfy curiosity, to be healed, to sit at the feet of this eloquent and controversial rabbi or simply to go along with the crowd. But at certain times during his ministry, Jesus challenged his would-be disciples with strong and sobering words about the cost of truly following him as Lord. As those who claim Jesus as our Lord, we too need to carefully weigh these words.

1. What about Jesus initially attracted you to him?

2. Read Luke 14:25-35. In verses 25-27, what does Jesus demand of those who would truly be his disciples?

3. The word *hate* (v. 26) is an obvious exaggeration for emphasis. In what sense are we to "hate" our family and even our own life?

4. A person carrying a cross in first-century Palestine was about to be executed. In this light, explain the meaning and implications of verse 27.

5. Imagine yourself building a tower (vv. 28-30). What types of costs would you need to consider before setting out to build?

What might keep you from finishing your task?

6. According to verses 31-32, what does the thoughtful king understand about battle?

7. What do these illustrations suggest about following Jesus (v. 33)?

8. Some have used verse 33 as a basis for renouncing ownership and for justifying an ascetic lifestyle or even monasticism. What is the difference between giving away everything that we have and "giving up" everything we have?

9. In New Testament times salt was used both as a preservative (to keep meat from rotting) and as a seasoning. How does this parallel our role as disciples of Jesus (vv. 34-35)?

10. How are those who do not wholeheartedly fulfill their commitment to follow Jesus like salt without saltiness?

11. Give some examples of how following Jesus could be costly for you. (Consider such areas as relationships, ambitions, finances, academics and so on.)

12. Are there areas of your life in which you are resisting Jesus' lordship? Explain.

What one thing is God calling you to change today?

4
Temptation

Genesis 39

Perhaps nothing so persistently plagues Christians like temptation. Abraham, David, Paul and even Jesus battled with it. In Genesis 39 we observe one man's struggle and victory over temptation. Joseph was the favored eleventh son of Jacob. His jealous brothers sold the seventeen-year-old Joseph into slavery. In Egypt he was again sold, this time to Potiphar, one of Pharaoh's officials. This passage recounts the first test for Joseph as God prepared him for the crucial role he would play in Israel's history.

1. How would you define the word *temptation?*

2. Read Genesis 39. How did Joseph come to be in charge of Potiphar's household (vv. 1-4)?

3. What were the results of Joseph being placed in this position (vv. 5-6)?

4. How might this position of authority, wealth and power have affected Joseph?

What do we learn about his character (vv. 7-9)?

5. Describe the character of Potiphar's wife (vv. 7-18).

What would have made her temptation especially difficult to resist?

6. Imagine yourself in Joseph's situation. Describe the mental, emotional and physical struggles you would experience.

7. What can you learn about overcoming persistent temptation from Joseph's example in verses 7-10?

8. When Potiphar's wife caught Joseph alone in the house, he ran out (v. 12). In what types of situations is it best to flee from temptation?

9. What price did Joseph pay for his obedience (vv. 13-20)?

10. What are the "Potiphar's wives" that persistently grab at your cloak and tempt you?

How might your refusal to succumb to them be costly?

11. What are some ways God has worked in your life to help you overcome temptation?

5
Faith

Genesis 22:1-19

Suppose God asked you to do something that seemed utterly foolish or even contrary to all that you understand God to be. How would you respond? For example, what if God asked you to kill your child? Unthinkable? Yet in Genesis 22 God places Abraham in just such a position. In this vivid and dramatic narrative, among the most beautiful in the Old Testament, we observe Abraham coming face to face with the supreme test of his faith in God.

1. How would you feel if God asked you to give up the most important person in your life?

2. Read Genesis 22:1-19. What words and phrases in verses 1-2 emphasize the extremely painful nature of God's command to Abraham?

3. Why would this command seem so incomprehensible to Abraham (see 17:15-22)?

4. If you were Abraham, what thoughts and feelings would you have during your three-day journey?

5. Recount the specific ways in which Abraham demonstrates faith in verses 1-8.

6. Imagine yourself as an onlooker during the drama of verses 6-8. Describe what you would see and hear.

7. How do Abraham's actions in verses 9-10 demonstrate the strength of his faith and the extent of his obedience?

8. In verses 11-18 the angel of the Lord calls out to Abraham twice. How would the angel's words and actions have deepened Abraham's faith?

9. From Abraham's example in this passage, how would you define faith?

What does this passage reveal about the relationship between faith and obedience?

10. Why do you think God tested Abraham?

What did Abraham learn about God from this experience?

11. What tests of faith are confronting you today?

12. How can Abraham's example encourage you to trust God more fully?

13. How did Abraham's faith have far-reaching consequences on other people (vv. 15-18)?

In what ways does your faith, or lack of it, affect people around you?

6
Holiness
Ephesians 4:17—5:7

For many people the word *holiness* conjures up images of a self-righteous person who is totally removed from the problems of the world, talks only about "spiritual things" and is serious and even sullen in appearance. Yet the New Testament word "holy" *(hagios)* is used to describe God's people in general and not a select few. It is the goal of the Christian's life and is fundamental to our witness and service in the world. Robert Murray McCheyne has rightly written that "a holy man is an awesome weapon in the hand of God." In this light, we need to recapture the biblical call to holy living.

1. People often view pastors, priests, missionaries and "full-time Christian workers" as more holy than other Christians. Why do you think this is so?

2. Read Ephesians 4:17—5:7. In verses 17-19 Paul describes how the Gentiles live. How does he characterize their minds, hearts and practices?

3. In contrast to the non-Christians described in verses 17-19, how were the Ephesians taught to live as Christians (vv. 20-24)?

4. Putting off our old self and putting on the new is a way of describing what happens when we become Christians. How does this description help us to understand the nature of conversion?

5. If you are to become like God in true righteousness and holiness (v. 24), why is it essential for you to "be made new in the attitude of your mind" (v. 23)?

In practical terms, what can we do to renew our minds?

6. Because of our new identity in Christ, what things must be put away, and what things ought to take their place (vv. 25-32)?

7. With each command in verses 25-32, explain the reason Paul calls us to live differently.

8. How can we imitate God and Christ in our relationships with others (5:1-2)?

9. Why is it "improper" and "out of place" for God's holy people to do the things mentioned in verses 3-4?

Which of these do you have the greatest difficulty avoiding? Explain.

10. What is Paul's warning about the person who claims to be a Christian but lives an immoral, impure or greedy life (vv. 5-7)?

11. Looking back over this passage, what different areas of our life are to be affected by holiness?

12. What type of behavior do you most need to put off and put on? What steps can you take to change this area of your life?

7
Compassion
Luke 10:25-37

All men will know that you are my disciples if you love one another." Tertullian, an early church theologian, boasted in one of his works that this statement of Jesus had become a fact. Even their enemies, writes Tertullian, marveled, saying, "Look how they love one another." But unfortunately the church has not always been marked by compassion and self-sacrifice. Far too often we speak of love but fail to back our words with deeds of kindness and mercy. We need to drink deeply from the simple but profound message of the story of the good Samaritan. Its familiarity has so weakened its impact that it is seen as an exception rather than the norm for the citizens of the kingdom of God. As you read this passage, imagine that you are hearing it from Jesus himself for the first time.

1. Think of a Christian you consider compassionate. What stands out to you about that person?

2. Read Luke 10:25-37. What do you learn in verses 25-29 about the expert in the law?

In particular, what does his reply to Jesus in verse 27 suggest about his knowledge of Scripture?

3. The expert in the law quotes from Deuteronomy 6:5 and Leviticus 19:18. How do these two commands summarize the essence of what God desires in our lives?

4. In reply to the question "Who is my neighbor?" Jesus tells a story (vv. 30-35). Describe a modern-day equivalent of this incident.

5. Suggest possible reasons why the priests and Levites may have passed by on the other side.

What are some ways we tend to pass by those in need?

6. Describe the Samaritan's involvement with the man from the moment he sees him (vv. 33-35).

Considering the racial and religious tensions that existed between Jews and Samaritans, why is the response of the Samaritan particularly surprising?

7. How have you personally been involved with people who are hurting financially, emotionally, physically or socially?

8. How does the extent of the Samaritan's involvement compare with most attempts we make to help needy people?

9. How has the story of the good Samaritan challenged the lawyer's understanding of "Love your neighbor as yourself" (vv. 36-37)?

10. What things keep you from not only seeing but also acting in response to the needs of those around you?

How can you begin to be more of a neighbor to these people?

8
Servanthood
Philippians 2

P ower. Glory. Success. Throughout human history these have captured the hearts of men and women. In the midst of a society which measures worth by position and wealth, it is no wonder that Christians have struggled to stand for the values of the kingdom of God: humility, self-denial, gentleness, love. In the eyes of the world these are often signs of weakness rather than strength. Yet in stark contrast to the values of our day, Jesus came not to be served but to serve. He calls us to follow in his steps.

1. What images come to your mind when you hear the word *servant?*

2. Read Philippians 2. How is verse 1 an incentive to obey Paul's commands in verse 2?

3. How do Paul's commands in verses 3-4 go against our natural tendencies?

How do they go against the spirit of our society?

4. How is Christ the supreme example of the humility and servanthood described in verses 3-4?

5. Considering Jesus' glory and majesty as God's equal, what did it cost him to be a servant (vv. 6-8)?

6. To what extent is your life characterized by this attitude of Christ Jesus?

7. In verses 12-18 Paul exhorts the Philippians to live godly lives. In what way is he a model of servanthood for them?

8. How does Paul contrast Timothy with others (vv. 20-21)?

9. If Timothy were alive today, how might his "genuine interest" in the church's welfare be manifested in practical ways?

10. How has Epaphroditus been a servant to Paul and the Philippians (vv. 25-30)?

11. How are Paul, Timothy and Epaphroditus examples of verses 3-5?

12. Jesus said, "The Son of Man did not come to be served, but to serve" (Mk 10:45). Paul, Timothy and Epaphroditus demonstrated the same kind of lifestyle. What are some ways you might follow their example more fully today or this week?

9
Self-Image
Exodus 3:1-15; 4:1-17

Few people today are immune to the effects of our fragmented, impersonal and fiercely competitive society. Many of us, both inside and outside the church, have been bruised by broken families and relationships. These wounds have not only damaged our self-images but have also hindered us from responding fully to God's love and purposes for our lives.

Moses, like many today, felt insignificant and inadequate. He had been raised in the courts of the king of Egypt in great wealth and with the best of education and training. But witnessing an act of unrighteousness against a fellow Jew, Moses took matters into his own hands and killed a man. As a result he was forced to flee to Midian, where he spent the next forty years herding sheep. At the beginning of Exodus 3, he is eighty years old and has accomplished very little in his life.

1. Why do you think so many people struggle with a poor self-image?

2. Read Exodus 3:1-15 and 4:1-17. Describe the setting in 3:1-3.

3. In 3:4 God calls Moses by name. What does this tell Moses about God?

4. Why does God send Moses to Pharaoh (3:7-10)?

5. In 3:11-15, Moses raises two objections against his going to Pharaoh. What do these objections reveal about Moses' view of himself and God?

6. In what situations do you feel inadequate to do what God commands or desires?

How can God's reply to Moses encourage you (3:12, 14-15)?

7. How is Moses' third objection in 4:1 understandable but inexcusable, especially in light of 3:18-20?

8. How does God reassure him in 4:2-9?

What are some of the resources God has given you to accomplish his will in a difficult or fearful area?

9. In verse 10 Moses claims that he lacks the gifts to serve God effectively. How does his view of himself differ from God's perspective (vv. 11-12)?

10. When is it legitimate to admit that we are unqualified for an area of service, and when is it merely a faithless excuse?

11. In what way can a poor self-image become sin (vv. 13-17)?

12. In what areas do you allow your self-image to be determined by your emotions or by other people rather than by God and his Word? Explain.

13. According to this passage, how should our self-image be affected by our image of God?

10
Spiritual Gifts and the Body of Christ
1 Corinthians 12:4-26

Tongues, prophecy, teaching, evangelism, mercy. In recent years a wide spectrum of views has developed among Christians about spiritual gifts. Charles Hummel describes a common misconception: "Traditional theology and American individualism have combined to foster a self-centered approach to spiritual gifts. Christians are often urged to enquire: 'What is *my* gift? How can I discover and use it?' Our culture pressures us to ask: 'Who am I? How can I be fulfilled and realize my potential?' " But is this the emphasis of the New Testament's teaching on spiritual gifts?

Similar questions and confusion about spiritual gifts prevailed in the church at Corinth. In 1 Corinthians 12—14 Paul discusses the nature, purpose and use of spiritual gifts as a corrective to the abuses which had arisen. 1 Corinthians 12:4-26 is particularly relevant to the church today.

1. In what ways can our entire body be hindered if one of its parts isn't functioning properly?

2. Read 1 Corinthians 12:4-26. In verses 4-11, what do we learn about the similarities and differences among spiritual gifts?

What is their purpose?

3. Why is the human body a good illustration of the body of Christ (vv. 12-13)?

4. What kinds of people today would make the statements Paul makes in verses 15-16?

5. How does Paul respond to these misconceptions (vv. 14-20)?

6. In contrast to the people portrayed in verses 14-16, how do the people described in verse 21 view themselves and those with less "spectacular" gifts?

7. In contrast to verse 21, how should we view and treat those who seem to be weaker or less honorable (vv. 22-23)?

Where do you see examples of this in your church or fellowship group?

8. Why would the "presentable parts" of the body need no special treatment (v. 24)?

9. If the more "spectacular" members of the body don't need special treatment, why are they usually the first to receive it?

10. How does this passage rebuke some of the clergy-laity distinctions prevalent in the church today?

11. Comment on your understanding of your own place in the body of Christ. For instance, do you feel inferior? Superior? Unsure of how you fit? Are you a lone ranger?

12. According to 12:7, each Christian is given gifts "for the common good" of the body. In this light, what can you be doing to build up your local church or fellowship group?

11
Humility
Mark 10:32-45

Pride comes in all shapes and sizes. Some of us put ourselves on a pedestal from which we judge the faults of everyone else. Others are so self-effacing that they cannot take their eyes off themselves and their own inadequacies. Still others swing like a pendulum from one extreme to the other. Paul exhorts us neither to exalt nor to belittle ourselves, but rather to think of ourselves with sober judgment (Rom 12:3). As we read in Mark 10:32-45, the disciples too were constantly learning to walk in humility like the Lord Jesus.

---

1. What is the difference between humility and a poor self-image?

---

2. Read Mark 10:32-45. What does Jesus tell his disciples about what awaits him in Jerusalem (vv. 32-34)?

3. In light of this news, how is the request of James and John inappropriate (v. 35)?

4. In what ways do you tend to be ambitious like James and John?

5. The words *baptism* and *cup* in verses 38-39 are sometimes used symbolically in Scripture to denote suffering. In this context, explain Jesus' reply to James and John.

6. Compare the sin of the other ten disciples with that of James and John (v. 41).

Have you ever felt envious or even indignant when others were honored and you were not? Explain.

7. How does Jesus contrast greatness in the world with greatness in God's kingdom (vv. 42-45)?

What is so radical about his definition of greatness?

8. In what ways do Christians today still embrace the world's concept of greatness?

9. Give a positive example of humility in action that you've seen in your church, family or work.

10. Jesus' concept of greatness and humility could transform every area of our lives. Name one way you could begin to follow his example.

12
Perseverance
2 Timothy 1:8—2:7

H ave you felt that following Jesus is much more demanding than you ever bargained for? Timothy had the same feelings. As a young and timid leader, he faced the dual dilemma of personal inadequacy and a problem-stricken church. If that weren't enough, Paul, his father in the faith, was in prison facing the prospect of death. His arrest evidently resulted in widespread defections from the faith. This is the last letter Paul wrote before he was executed. From his cell, he challenges Timothy to endure.

1. Have you ever felt like giving up Christianity and returning to an easier way of life? Explain.

2. Read 2 Timothy 1:8—2:7. Why might Timothy be ashamed to testify about the Lord, or be ashamed of Paul (v. 8)?

3. After calling Timothy to suffer with him for the gospel, what specific truths does Paul focus on (1:9-10)?

Why do you think he reminds Timothy of these at this particular point in the letter?

4. How does the message of the gospel encourage you to stand firm when you are tempted to be ashamed of Christ or of another Christian?

5. What do verses 13-14 suggest about the difficulties Timothy will encounter?

How does Paul's own experience support the probability that Timothy will face difficulties?

6. Imagine yourself in Paul's position—alone, imprisoned, deserted by "everyone in the province of Asia" (1:15). How do you think you would react?

Would you also be tempted to desert? Explain.

7. What is distinctive about Onesiphorus (1:16-18)?

8. Against the background of Paul's impending death and the disloyalty of the Asian church, what is the significance of Paul's command in 2:2?

9. Reflect on the three metaphors describing the Christian life (2:3-6). How does each provide insight into the life of a disciple?

10. In each illustration, what are the consequences for the person who fails to endure?

11. In what specific ways might it cost you to endure for the sake of the gospel, both now and throughout your life?

12. Timothy was undoubtedly overwhelmed by his own inadequacy and the massive defections from the church. How would 2:1 encourage him in the face of the great task at hand?

How is it an encouragement to you?

Leader's Notes

Leading a Bible discussion can be an enjoyable and rewarding experience. But it can also be *scary*—especially if you've never done it before. If this is your feeling, you're in good company. When God asked Moses to lead the Israelites out of Egypt, he replied, "O Lord, please send someone else to do it!" (Ex 4:13).

When Solomon became king of Israel, he felt the task was far beyond his abilities. "I am only a little child and do not know how to carry out my duties. . . . Who is able to govern this great people of yours?" (1 Kings 3:7, 9).

When God called Jeremiah to be a prophet, he replied, "Ah, Sovereign LORD, . . . I do not know how to speak; I am only a child" (Jer 1:6).

The list goes on. The apostles were "unschooled, ordinary men" (Acts 4:13). Timothy was young, frail and frightened. Paul's "thorn in the flesh" made him feel weak. But God's response to all of his servants—including you—is essentially the same: "My grace is sufficient for you" (2 Cor 12:9). Relax. God helped these people in spite of their weaknesses, and he can help you in spite of your feelings of inadequacy.

There is another reason why you should feel encouraged. Leading a Bible discussion is not difficult if you follow certain guidelines. You don't need to be an expert on the Bible or a trained teacher. The suggestions listed below should enable you to effectively and enjoyably fulfill your role as leader.

Preparing to Lead

1. Ask God to help you understand and apply the passage to your own life. Unless this happens, you will not be prepared to lead others. Pray too for the various members of the group. Ask God to give you an enjoyable and profitable time together studying his Word.

2. As you begin each study, read and reread the assigned Bible passage to familiarize yourself with what the author is saying. In the case of book studies, you may want to read through the entire book prior to the first study. This will give you a helpful overview of its contents.

3. This study guide is based on the New International Version of the Bible. It will help you and the group if you use this translation as the basis for your study and discussion. Encourage others to use the NIV also, but allow them the freedom to use whatever translation they prefer.

4. Carefully work through each question in the study. Spend time in meditation and reflection as you formulate your answers.

5. Write your answers in the space provided in the study guide. This will help you to express your understanding of the passage clearly.

6. It might help you to have a Bible dictionary handy. Use it to look up any unfamiliar words, names or places. (For additional help on how to study a passage, see chapter five of *Leading Bible Discussions,* IVP.)

7. Once you have finished your own study of the passage, familiarize yourself with the leader's notes for the study you are leading. These are designed to help you in several ways. First, they tell you the purpose the study guide author had in mind while writing the study. Take time to think through how the study questions work together to accomplish that purpose. Second, the notes provide you with additional background information or comments on some of the questions. This information can be useful if people have difficulty understanding or answering a question. Third, the leader's notes can alert you to potential problems you may encounter during the study.

8. If you wish to remind yourself of anything mentioned in the leader's notes, make a note to yourself below that question in the study.

Leading the Study

1. Begin the study on time. Unless you are leading an evangelistic Bible study, open with prayer, asking God to help you to understand and apply the passage.

2. Be sure that everyone in your group has a study guide. Encourage them to prepare beforehand for each discussion by working through the questions in the guide.

3. At the beginning of your first time together, explain that these studies are meant to be discussions not lectures. Encourage the members of the group to participate. However, do not put pressure on those who may be hesitant to speak during the first few sessions.

4. Read the introductory paragraph at the beginning of the discussion. This will orient the group to the passage being studied.

5. Read the passage aloud if you are studying one chapter or less. You may choose to do this yourself, or someone else may read if he or she has been asked to do so prior to the study. Longer passages may occasionally be read in parts at different times during the study. Some studies may cover several chapters. In such cases reading aloud would probably take too much time, so the group members should simply read the assigned passages prior to the study.

6. As you begin to ask the questions in the guide, keep several things in mind. First, the questions are designed to be used just as they are written. If you wish, you may simply read them aloud to the group. Or you may prefer to express them in your own words. However, unnecessary rewording of the questions is not recommended.

Second, the questions are intended to guide the group toward understanding and applying the *main idea* of the passage. The author of the guide has stated his or her view of this central idea in the *purpose* of the study in the leader's notes. You should try to understand how the passage expresses this idea and how the study questions work together to lead the group in that direction.

There may be times when it is appropriate to deviate from the study guide. For example, a question may have already been answered. If so, move on to the next question. Or someone may raise an important question not covered in the guide. Take time to discuss it! The important thing is to use discretion. There may be many routes you can travel to reach the goal of the study. But the easiest route is usually the one the author has suggested.

7. Avoid answering your own questions. If necessary, repeat or rephrase them until they are clearly understood. An eager group quickly becomes passive and silent if they think the leader will do most of the talking.

8. Don't be afraid of silence. People may need time to think about the question before formulating their answers.

9. Don't be content with just one answer. Ask, "What do the rest of you think?" or "Anything else?" until several people have given answers to the question.

10. Acknowledge all contributions. Try to be affirming whenever possible. Never reject an answer. If it is clearly wrong, ask, "Which verse led you to that conclusion?" or again, "What do the rest of you think?"

11. Don't expect every answer to be addressed to you, even though this will probably happen at first. As group members become more at ease, they will begin to truly interact with each other. This is one sign of a healthy discussion.

12. Don't be afraid of controversy. It can be very stimulating. If you don't resolve an issue completely, don't be frustrated. Move on and keep it in mind for later. A subsequent study may solve the problem.

13. Stick to the passage under consideration. It should be the source for answering the questions. Discourage the group from unnecessary cross-referencing. Likewise, stick to the subject and avoid going off on tangents.

14. Periodically summarize what the *group* has said about the passage. This helps to draw together the various ideas mentioned and gives continuity to the study. But don't preach.

15. Conclude your time together with conversational prayer. Be sure to ask God's help to apply those things which you learned in the study.

16. End on time.

Many more suggestions and helps are found in *Leading Bible Discussions* (IVP). Reading and studying through that would be well worth your time.

Components of Small Groups
A healthy small group should do more than study the Bible. There are four components you should consider as you structure your time together.

Nurture. Being a part of a small group should be a nurturing and edifying experience. You should grow in your knowledge and love of God and each other. If we are to properly love God, we must know and keep his commandments (Jn 14:15). That is why Bible study should be a foundational part of your small group. But you can be nurtured by other things as well. You can memorize Scripture, read and discuss a book, or occasionally listen to a tape of a good speaker.

Community. Most people have a need for close friendships. Your small group can be an excellent place to cultivate such relationships. Allow time for informal interaction before and after the study. Have a time of sharing during the meeting. Do fun things together as a group, such as a potluck supper or a picnic. Have someone bring refreshments to the meeting. Be creative!

Worship. A portion of your time together can be spent in worship and prayer. Praise God together for who he is. Thank him for what he has done and is doing in your lives and in the world. Pray for each other's needs. Ask God to help you to apply what you have learned. Sing hymns together.

Mission. Many small groups decide to work together in some form of outreach. This can be a practical way of applying what you have learned. You can host a series of evangelistic discussions for your friends or neighbors. You can visit people at a home for the elderly. Help a widow with cleaning or repair jobs around her home. Such projects can have a transforming influence on your group.

For a detailed discussion of the nature and function of small groups, read *Small Group Leaders' Handbook* or *Good Things Come in Small Groups* (both from IVP).

Study 1. Justification: The Meaning of the Cross. Romans 3:9-26.
Purpose: To understand why God accepts us and how this acceptance should affect our attitude toward ourselves, others and God.
Question 1. Almost every study begins with an "approach" question, which is meant to be asked *before* the passage is read. These questions are important for several reasons.

First, they help the group to warm up to each other. No matter how well a group may know each other or how comfortable they may be with each other, there is always a stiffness that needs to be overcome before people will begin to talk openly. A good question will break the ice.

Second, approach questions get people thinking along the lines of the topic of the study. Most people will have lots of different things going on in their minds (dinner, an important meeting coming up, how to get the car fixed) that will have nothing to do with the study. A creative question will get their attention and draw them into the discussion.

Third, approach questions can reveal where our thoughts or feelings need to be transformed by Scripture. This is why it is especially important *not* to read the passage before the approach question is asked. The passage will tend to color the honest reactions people would otherwise give because they are of course *supposed* to think the way the Bible does. Giving honest responses to various issues before they find out what the Bible says may help them to see where their thoughts or attitudes need to be changed.

The purpose of this specific question is to help people recognize subtle ways in which they live by works rather than by grace. Help people to clarify or expand on their answers. For example, after we sin we sometimes try to make payment for that sin ourselves, perhaps by spending an extra half-hour in prayer, doing an "extra" good deed, and so on.
Question 2. It might be helpful to understand the context of this study. In Romans 1:18—3:20 Paul describes everyone's condition apart from Jesus Christ. These chapters demonstrate that "no one will be declared righteous in his [God's] sight by observing the law" (3:20). Then in 3:21—5:21 Paul

describes the "righteousness from God [which] comes through faith in Jesus Christ" (3:22).

Paul's portrait is drawn from the characteristics of humanity in general. Not everyone has reached the depths of depravity described here, but everyone is capable of reaching such depths because our nature is fallen.

Question 3. The group may have already answered this question while discussing question 2. If so, move on to the next question. However, their answer to question 2 may have been fairly general. Question 3 allows them to be more specific as they look at Paul's portrait of fallen humanity.

Question 6. Questions 6-10 will look at each of these words, one at a time. In question 6 you only need to discuss the meaning of *faith.*

Verses 21-26 are central to the study. You need to understand and be gripped by the deep significance of the cross if you expect it to make an impact on others. A Bible dictionary can help you define key words.

Question 8. Help the group to see the connection between God's high view of us in Christ and how we ought to view ourselves.

Question 10. Some people object to the idea of God's wrath being turned away by the death of a sacrificial victim. In their opinion this makes God too similar to pagan deities who could be bribed. Yet in paganism the worshiper tries desperately to appease the god's wrath. In Christianity God himself graciously provided and even became the sacrificial victim.

Question 11. Ask the group to first consider our relationships with one another, then our relationship with God.

Study 2.   The Lordship of Jesus Christ (Part 1). Colossians 1:15-23.
Purpose: To understand the significance of the person and work of Christ.
Question 1. If several people in your group became Christians as children, you might want to change the question to, "How do you think your non-Christian friends view Jesus Christ?"
Question 2. Concerning Christ's incarnation, F. F. Bruce writes: "It may be observed in passing that there is a close association between the doctrine of man's creation in the divine image and the doctrine of our Lord's incarnation; it is because man in the creative order bears the image of his Creator that it was possible for the Son of God to become incarnate as man and in His humanity to display the glory of the invisible God" (F. F. Bruce, *Ephesians and Colossians* in The New International Commentary on the New Testament, ed. F. F. Bruce [Grand Rapids, Mich.: Eerdmans, 1973], p. 194).
Question 3. The term *firstborn* is commonly used to mean "supreme" or "sovereign." It is a synonym for "most exalted of the kings of the earth" (see Ps 89:27).

Question 5. Many people know that all things were created by Jesus Christ and for him, but few have meditated on the personal implications of this fact. If the group needs help with the second part of the question, you might point them to Christ's ownership of all creation—including us—and what this suggests about our rights.

Question 9. Be sure to leave time for this question. It helps the group to apply the main theme of the passage.

Question 10. Someone may raise a question as to whether verse 23 is teaching that we can lose our salvation. While Paul is confident that the Colossians will remain firm in the faith, he inserts a conditional clause to emphasize their need to persevere. The thrust of the Bible teaches that all true Christians will endure to the end. However, this passage and others indicate that believers are not immune to the dangers of apostasy.

Study 3.   The Lordship of Jesus Christ (Part 2). Luke 14:25-35.

Purpose: To evaluate one's life in light of the lordship of Christ and to give Christ control of one uncommitted area.

The IVP booklet *My Heart—Christ's Home* is a helpful introduction to this study and to the topic itself. You might read it yourself before the study and recommend it to the group for further consideration.

Question 3. Matthew 10:37 helps to clarify Jesus' meaning in Luke 14:26: "Anyone who loves his father or mother more than me is not worthy of me; anyone who loves his son or daughter more than me is not worthy of me." Jesus demands to have first place in all our relationships.

Question 4. The New Testament makes it clear that suffering comes before glory, that the cross comes before the crown. In Jesus' words, we must be willing to lose our lives for his sake—that is, give up all claim to our possessions, our relationships, our ambitions and even our own lives—if we want to follow him. This must be done daily, not just once (Lk 9:23). Only then will we find life. The cost of commitment will be discussed more fully in the rest of the study, so don't feel that you must cover everything here.

Question 7. The main point of these illustrations is that we should carefully consider the cost of following Jesus before we become his disciples. Help the group to focus primarily on this idea. If they begin to go off on a tangent, ask them: "What is the main point of these illustrations? How does it relate to following Jesus?"

Question 8. There are two extremes to avoid in applying this verse. One is a wooden literalism followed by many cults. They suggest that Christ commands us to give away all our possessions and to renounce our family, friends, career and so on. Another extreme is to so spiritualize Christ's words that they are emptied of their force. Following Christ costs us everything in principle but nothing in practice! Help the group to avoid these extremes and to wrestle with the true meaning of Jesus' words.

Questions 11-12. Help the group to be specific in considering the implications of Christ's lordship. Encourage each person to identify one area which God is calling him or her to change.

Study 4. Temptation. Genesis 39.

Purpose: To consider the sources of temptation and how to effectively combat them.

One problem you may face in this study is an unwillingness on the part of the group members to be really open about their struggles with temptation. Seek to create an open, accepting atmosphere. To do this you will need to be open about your own struggles with temptation. However, be careful not to put others on the spot if they are not ready to share.

Question 1. *The American Heritage Dictionary* defines *tempt* as follows: "To entice (someone) to commit an unwise or immoral act, esp. by a promise of reward." If the group has difficulty answering this question, you might read this definition.

Question 9. Although Joseph's imprisonment is costly and seems to be only negative at the outset, it might be noted that in Genesis 40—50 God uses this seemingly adverse situation to accomplish greater purposes through Joseph. See, for example, Genesis 50:20.

Question 10. There is often an even greater cost when we give in to temptation. David's sin with Bathsheba and subsequent murder in 2 Samuel 11 is a poignant example of the consequences of yielding to temptation. Although David was forgiven his sin, the kingdom of Israel was never the same after that. You may want to remind the group of this account for illustration.

Question 11. Encourage the group to be specific in answering this question. You may want to remind them of God's assurance to us in 1 Corinthians 10:13 as we face temptation.

Study 5. Faith. Genesis 22:1-19.

Purpose: To understand the nature of faith and to be encouraged to trust God more fully.

Question 3. Take adequate time for this question. Be sure the group grasps the twofold struggle of Abraham: (1) God's command seemed to conflict with his previous promise that through Isaac the great nation of Israel would be born, and (2) his personal struggle with sacrificing his only son (vv. 2, 12, 16) for whom he had waited so many years.

Questions 4 and 6. Encourage members of the group to be creative and enter into the drama as deeply as possible.

Question 9. Hebrews 11:1 defines faith as "being sure of what we hope for and certain of what we do not see." Faith can also be described as believing and trusting that what God says is true and acting accordingly.

Questions 11-12. Leave time for these key application questions. Attempt to think through, in advance, the various tests of faith which confront you and the members of your group during a typical week. For example, what does it mean to act in faith when a tragedy occurs, when you are tempted to sin, when you face financial difficulties or when you are ridiculed for being a Christian?

Study 6.   Holiness. Ephesians 4:17—5:7.

Purpose: To understand our call to holiness and to be motivated toward godly living.

It might be helpful for your group if you place this passage in its context. John Stott writes: "For three chapters Paul has been unfolding for his readers the eternal purpose of God being worked out in history. . . . Paul sees an alienated humanity being reconciled, a fractured humanity being united, even a new humanity being created. . . . Now the apostle moves on from the new society to the new standards which are expected of it. So he turns from exposition to exhortation, from what God has done . . . to what we must do" (*The Message of Ephesians* [Downers Grove, Ill.: InterVarsity Press, 1979], p. 146).

Question 3. The word *holy* in Scripture usually refers to a person or thing which has been set apart for God and his service. It also denotes the purity of God's character and, secondarily, the character of his people.

Question 4. The RSV mistakenly translates *put off* and *put on* as commands. In fact, Paul is not commanding us but rather is describing what we were taught, presumably at conversion. The parallel passage in Colossians says, "Do not lie to each other, since you *have* taken off your old self with its practices and *have* put on the new self" (Col 3:9-10, our emphasis). Because we have put off the old self and put on the new, we are commanded to live differently.

Question 5. This question relates to the issue of self-image. Our view of ourselves very much influences the way we act. Paul's argument here is that because of what God has done in Jesus Christ, we are new people with new identities. Therefore, we should be leading a radically different life than we were prior to conversion.

The second part of question 5 could lead to an entirely different discussion on claiming God's promises, meditating on Scripture, and so on. While these are important points for consideration, don't spend too much time on them. Remember that the focus of the study is holiness.

Question 8. Be sure to allow enough time to consider this question fully. People often fail to see that holiness should affect our relationships with others.

Question 10. Some members of your group may be troubled by Paul's warning. If we are saved by faith and not by works (2:8-9), then how could our works exclude us from God's kingdom? Paul's point is that people who live such lives give evidence that they are not God's children, regardless of what they claim.

Study 7. Compassion. Luke 10:25-37.

Purpose: To understand the biblical nature of compassion and to consider how to become a better neighbor in at least one specific situation.

Question 2. An "expert in the law" or "lawyer," as it appears in some translations, was not an expert on the secular law but on the first five books of the Old Testament and their application to secular affairs.

Question 4. The road from Jerusalem to Jericho was about seventeen miles long. It was rocky and treacherous and known for its dangers to travelers at the hands of robbers.

Question 5. You might want to mention that touching a dead person was forbidden by the ceremonial law (Lev 21:1-4). Some commentators have suggested that this may have had some bearing on their negligence. This, of course, relates to the tension between our remaining separate from the world while a part of it. However, there are many other possible explanations.

Question 6. During New Testament times there was considerable hostility between Jews and Samaritans. The Jews considered the Samaritans racially and religiously impure. The Samaritans accepted only the first five books of the Old Testament (with some of their own changes). They built a rival temple on Mount Gerizim which the Jews destroyed in 128 B.C. Between A.D. 6 and 9 the Samaritans scattered bones in the Jerusalem temple during Passover (bones were considered unclean). As a result of these tensions, John 4:9 states, "Jews do not associate with Samaritans." In fact, they would normally walk around Samaria rather than take the shorter route through it. All of these things help us to feel the impact of Jesus' story about the good Samaritan.

Question 8. In this question it would be easy to focus exclusively on our failures. Avoid this tendency by encouraging the group to also share positive examples of obedience from their own experience.

Question 10. Again, pace yourself well so that these critical questions of application are fully considered and the truths of the passage fully digested.

Study 8.   Servanthood. Philippians 2.

Purpose: To understand the biblical concept of servanthood so that we may better serve others.

Question 4. Verses 5-11 contain one of the most beautiful portraits of Christ found in Scripture. It is astonishing that God would be willing to become a man. It is equally surprising that he would take the form of a lowly servant rather than a wealthy monarch. But it is incomprehensible that he would be willing to be utterly humiliated by dying in the manner reserved for the worst of criminals. These few verses capture the greatness of Christ's humility and love.

Question 5. This question may or may not overlap with the previous question, depending on how fully the group answers question 4. If there is significant overlap, simply move on to the next question.

Question 6. This question is designed to allow for self-examination. The group need not spend time thinking about specific ways to cultivate a servant's attitude, since this will be discussed later in the study (see questions 8 and 12).

Question 7. It is important to realize that Paul is writing this letter from prison. As a result of his service to Jesus Christ and the church, he is confined under guard (possibly in Rome) and may be facing the threat of execution.

Question 12. Encourage each member of the group to think of practical ways he or she can serve others during the coming week. Perhaps the group can share their experiences in applying this study at the beginning of the next study.

Study 9.   Self-Image. Exodus 3:1-15; 4:1-17.

Purpose: To understand how our self-image must be balanced by a proper image of God.

It will help you if you understand the approach of this passage and this study. In a sense, this is not a typical study on self-image. Normally such studies attempt to replace low self-esteem by giving us reasons for high self-esteem: we are created in God's image, we are loved and valued by God, and so on. It is important for us to grasp these things. But this passage and study take a different approach. God does not seek to correct Moses' low self-image by giving him a proper image of *self,* but rather by giving him a proper image of *God.* Because God is with him, Moses' weaknesses and sense of inadequacy are not obstacles but opportunities to witness God's power, grace and sufficiency.

Question 6. Help the group to identify with Moses. God was calling him to an awesome task which was far beyond his capabilities. Someone in your group may be in a similar situation.

Question 11. Don't be satisfied with one simple answer to this question. Have the group explore other possibilities. A poor self-image can lead to different types of sins: false humility which is a form of pride, an avoidance of biblical fellowship, disobedience and so on. Also, be sure to take into account the complex factors which cause someone to have a poor self-image, some of which are unrelated to a person's spiritual state.

Question 12. A healthy self-image is not synonymous with self-confidence or self-sufficiency. Our confidence and sufficiency should be in God and his Word. Likewise, Moses' self-image needed to be tempered by a healthy image of God and by his promise "I will be with you."

Study 10.   Spiritual Gifts and the Body of Christ. 1 Corinthians 12:4-26.

Purpose: To understand the nature and importance of spiritual gifts in order to more effectively serve and build up the body of Christ.

This is a hot issue! There may be someone in your group who insists on the priority of such gifts as tongues, prophecy and healing today. Others may deny their existence altogether, while still others may be completely ignorant of spiritual gifts. A thorough and balanced treatment of spiritual gifts is found in Charles Hummel's *Fire in the Fireplace* (Downers Grove, Ill.: InterVarsity Press, 1978). As you lead the discussion, be sensitive to the different positions within your group. It is essential, however, that you help the group to stick to the passage and understand what *this* text is actually teaching. Although this is not by any means an exhaustive treatment of spiritual gifts, it provides a necessary foundation for any further consideration of the topic.

It is also important to realize the nature of this study. It asks questions which deliberately avoid the more controversial aspects of the passage. It focuses instead on those areas which are relevant to all Christians, regardless of their views of spiritual gifts.

Question 2. Some members of your group may be completely ignorant of spiritual gifts. If they ask for a definition at the beginning of the study, tell them that the study itself will help them to understand the nature and purpose of spiritual gifts.

Question 10. Don't let this question turn into an antileadership gripe session. While the Bible affirms the priesthood of all believers, God has clearly placed certain people in positions of responsibility and leadership over his church (Eph 4:11).

Question 11. Some people may be reluctant to share their real feelings, especially if they see themselves as inferior or outsiders in any way. This can be an opportunity to affirm them and build fellowship within your group. Be prepared to spend some time on this.

Question 12. Some of the members of your group may wish to do further study about spiritual gifts. You might mention that there are four primary passages in Scripture where spiritual gifts are discussed: Romans 12, 1 Corinthians 12, Ephesians 4 and 1 Peter 4. Each of these contributes to our overall understanding of spiritual gifts.

Study 11. Humility. Mark 10:32-45

Purposes: To recognize the biblical model of humility and the dangers of pride. To begin renewing our minds and lives in accordance with Jesus' teaching and example.

Question 3. James and John were so concerned about themselves that they failed to hear what Jesus was saying. His words didn't fit all the dreams they hoped would be realized when they reached Jerusalem. They still imagined that Jesus would overthrow the Romans and the corrupt religious leaders and establish his glorious kingdom. When this happened, they expected to be given positions of power, prestige and authority. No wonder their world was turned upside down a few days later!

Question 4. Some group members may feel they don't have a problem with ambition. You might ask them whether they desire recognition, power, prestige or authority.

Question 5. This passage, and especially this verse, takes on added significance when one considers the background of this Gospel. It was written during the reign of the emperor Nero to the Christian community in Rome facing suffering and martyrdom. If time allows, you may want to raise the question of how these words would have been especially relevant for such an audience.

Question 6. The disciples evidently felt that cabinet posts would not be assigned until they reached Jerusalem. They were angry primarily because they thought James and John might have been given the best positions.

Question 7. Help the group to see that Jesus stands the world's concept of greatness on its head. Those who are on the top are really on the bottom, and those who are on the bottom may truly be at the top!

Question 8. Don't let the discussion turn into a gossip session. The goal is to see the prevalence and destructive effects of pride within the Christian community.

Question 10. This question is specific in order to allow people to begin following Christ's example in at least one area. However, as the group discusses this question, people will hear several ideas they can put into practice.

Study 12.   Perseverance. 2 Timothy 1:8—2:7.

Purpose: To understand the importance of perseverance in the face of suffering and difficulty.

Question 2. It is important to note that Paul is not only calling Timothy to be unashamed of Jesus but also to be unashamed of Paul himself. Why? Because along with Jesus, Paul has been mocked and deserted and is now in prison for his faith. His arrest has made following Christ far less attractive. Nevertheless, Timothy is called to identify unabashedly with Jesus, Paul and the church.

Question 4. Someone may raise the question, "Shouldn't I keep my distance from a Christian who is standing for issues or advocating methods with which I disagree?" You may want to point the group to Jesus' response to the disciples in Luke 9:49-50 where the disciples were faced with a similar temptation.

Question 9. Don't let the discussion drift to a debate over such things as the exact nature of the victor's crown (v. 5) or the share of the crops (v. 6). These are not Paul's primary points. Rather he emphasizes that faithful obedience and strenuous labor are necessary for persevering as a disciple of Jesus Christ. For a fuller discussion of the topic see John Stott's *The Message of 2 Timothy* (Downers Grove, Ill.: InterVarsity Press, 1973).

Question 11. You may want to encourage the group to imagine their lives ten or twenty years down the road.

Andrea Sterk, a former InterVarsity campus staff member, is pursuing Ph.D. studies in church history. Peter Scazzero, also a former InterVarsity staff member, is pastor of Community Alliance Church in New York City.